Airliners of East and Central Asia

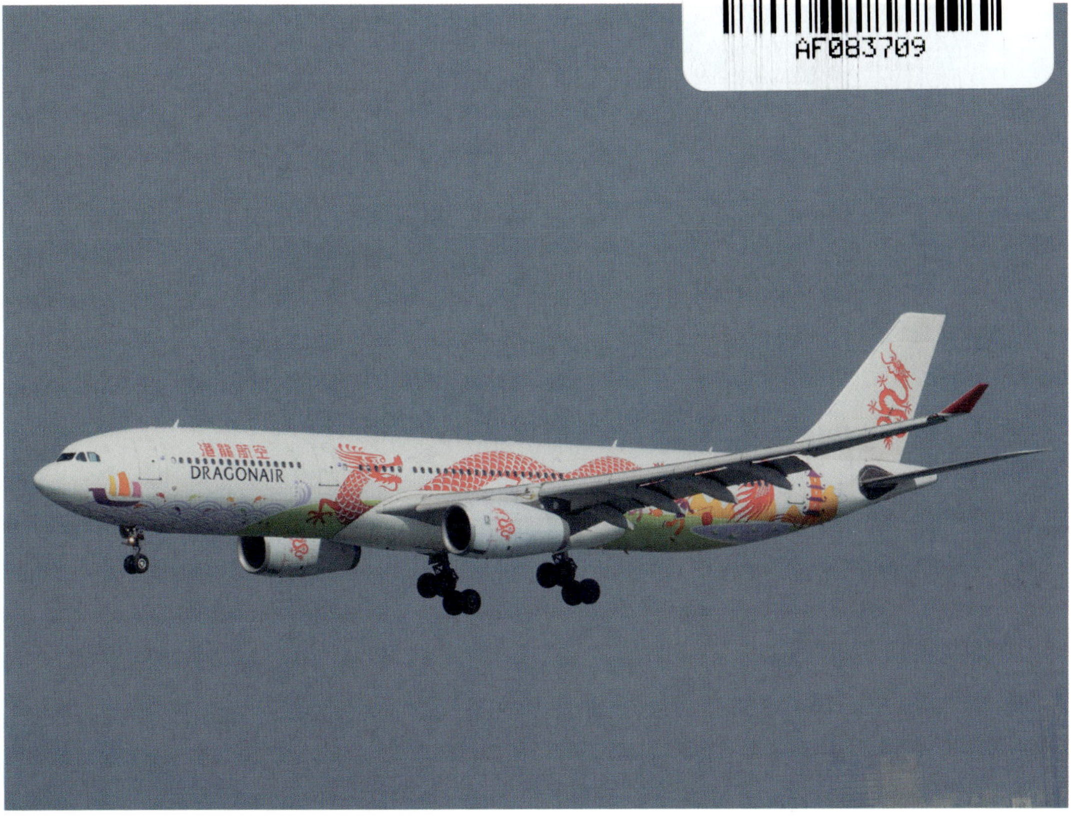

GERRY MANNING

KEY Books

MODERN COMMERCIAL AIRCRAFT SERIES, VOLUME 1

Published by Key Books
An imprint of Key Publishing Ltd
PO Box 100
Stamford
Lincs PE9 1XQ

www.keypublishing.com

The right of Gerry Manning to be identified as the author of this book has been asserted in accordance with the Copyright, Designs and Patents Act 1988 Sections 77 and 78.

Copyright © Gerry Manning, 2022

ISBN 978 1 80282 353 0

All rights reserved. Reproduction in whole or in part in any form whatsoever or by any means is strictly prohibited without the prior permission of the Publisher.

Typeset by SJmagic DESIGN SERVICES, India.

Introduction

The aim of this book is to illustrate the different types of aircraft, and the airlines that fly them, in one geographical area of the huge continent of Asia. The countries covered, in this volume, are China (including Hong Kong and Macau), Taiwan, Japan, South Korea, North Korea (Democratic People's Republic of Korea), Mongolia, Uzbekistan, Kazakhstan, Tajikistan, Kyrgyzstan and Turkmenistan.

In some cases, with different airlines, I have tried to show the variations of types that these operators fly, as a single picture cannot do justice to the many types of aircraft that some carriers operate on long-, medium- and short-haul routes.

All the pictures are my own, having been taken on my travels, and are a mix of digital images and scanned Fujichrome slides.

Gerry Manning
Liverpool
August 2022

Tails of Japan. A trio of All Nippon Airways (ANA) airliners are at their gates at Hong Kong Chek Lap Kok Airport, awaiting their next sets of passengers for the return flights to the Japanese cities they operate from.

Airliners of East and Central Asia

The Boeing 727 first flew in February 1963 and was the first jet airliner to sell over 1000 airframes. Pictured at Beijing Capital International Airport, China, in October 1999, is Boeing 727-281 JU-1037 c/n 20573 of MIAT-Mongolian Airlines. Based in the Mongolian capital of Ulaanbaatar, it is the flag carrier for the land-locked nation.

At one time, the Boeing 737 was the top selling jet airliner in the world. The original -100 first took to the air in April 1967. Since then, it has progressed to the -900 and the MAX variants, as well as military versions. Pictured on approach to Xi'an Xianyang International Airport, in November 2012, is Boeing 737-86J B-5361 c/n 30063 of Shenzhen Airlines. Based in the city of the same name, the carrier's main operations are in the south of China.

Xiamen Air Boeing 737-85C B-5659 c/n 38396 is seen about to land at Xi'an Xianyang International Airport in November 2012. Operating from its base in the city Xiamen, the airline operates to over 50 cities.

Korean Air is the Seoul-based flag carrier for the Republic of Korea. It flies to over 100 locations in worldwide operations. About to land at Xi'an Xianyang International Airport, in November 2012, is Boeing 737-8Q8 HL8243 c/n 38825.

Shanghai Airlines Boeing 737-8Q8 B-2168 c/n 30632 lines up to land at Xi'an Xianyang International Airport in November 2012. The airline operates scheduled services on both domestic and international routes from its base in the largest city in China.

Based in the port city of Tianjin, Okay Airways operates mainly domestic passenger, charter and cargo operations. Landing at Xi'an Xianyang International Airport, in November 2012, is Boeing 737-8A5 B-5578 c/n 33560. Note the name on the cabin roof is shortened to just OK Air.

Founded in 1994, by the local provincial government, Shandong Airlines (SDA) is based in the city of Jinan. It is basically a domestic scheduled carrier but with some regional international routes. Boeing 737-85N B-5649 c/n 38640 is landing at Xi'an Xianyang International Airport in November 2012.

China Xinhua Airlines is one of the subsidiaries of Hainan Airlines. Its main operating bases are at Beijing and Tianjin. Boeing 737-883 B-5082 c/n 29640 is on approach to Xi'an Xianyang International Airport in November 2012. Like all the subsidiaries, it has its own name on the cabin roof, but all have the same tail markings.

It is not uncommon for Chinese carriers to have their aircraft in special liveries. Pictured about to land at Beijing Capital International Airport, in November 2012, is Boeing 737-89L B-2642 c/n 29877 of the nation's flag carrier, Air China.

Dalian Airlines Boeing 737-89L B-5639 c/n 40033 is on approach to land at Beijing Capital International Airport in November 2012. The airline is based in the northeastern port city of Dalian and operates domestic passenger services.

Japan's flag carrier is Japan Airlines (JAL). It operates worldwide and also operates a full domestic service. Pictured about to depart on an internal service at Miyazaki Airport, in October 2014, is Boeing 737-846 JA318J c/n 35347.

The other large carrier in Japan is All Nippon Airways. Like Japan Airlines, it operates an extensive international and domestic passenger service, as well as cargo operations. Seen arriving at Miyazaki Airport, in October 2014, is Boeing 737-881 JA51AN c/n 33886. As well as its All Nippon Airways livery, it shows off the fact that the carrier is a member of the Star Alliance group of airlines.

Pictured taking off from Ibaraki Hyakuri Airport, in October 2014, on a domestic service is Skymark Airlines Boeing 737-81D JA73NQ c/n 39432. Based at Tokyo Haneda Airport, the airline operates scheduled passenger services between major cities.

Solaseed Air is a Japanese low-cost carrier operating between key cities in the country. Pictured taking off from Miyazaki Airport, in October 2014, is Boeing 737-81D JA808X c/n 39433.

Service Cargo Air Transport (SCAT) is a Kazakhstan-based carrier operating a mix of passenger and cargo flights around that vast country, as well as neighbouring nations. Seen at Astana International Airport, in June 2016, is Boeing 737-522 LY-AWD c/n 26739. This aircraft is leased, hence its Lithuanian registration.

On approach to land at Hong Kong Chek Lap Kok Airport, in January 2013, is Boeing 737-86N HL7555 c/n 30230 of Jin Air. Seoul-based, it is a low-cost subsidiary of Korean Air and operates both domestic and regional international services.

Boeing 737-8FH B-5115 c/n 29640 is pictured about to land at the new Guangzhou Baiyun Airport in November 2012. The aircraft is operated by Xi'an-based Chang An Airlines, which is part of the Hainan Airlines group. It has since been rebranded as Air Changan.

Jeju Air was the first low-cost carrier in the Republic of Korea. It operates both domestic and regional international services from the city of Jeju. Seen on approach to Hong Kong Chek Lap Kok Airport, in January 2013, is Boeing 737-86J HL8206 c/n 30877.

Set up in 2004, Hong Kong Express Airways was acquired by the Hainan Airlines group two years later. Pictured on approach to its home base, in January 2013, is Boeing 737-8Q8 B-KBR c/n 35276. The airline has since been taken over by Cathay Pacific Airways and operates as HK Express.

Shanghai-based China Eastern Airlines is one of the largest carriers in that nation, with both domestic and worldwide international scheduled services. Boeing 737-79P B-5225 c/n 33045 is seen on approach to Hong Kong Chek Lap Kok Airport in January 2013.

Taking off from Runway 01R at Bangkok Suvarnabhumi Airport, in November 2010, is Boeing 737-809 B-18610 c/n 29105, in the colourful livery of China Airlines. It is the flag carrier for Taiwan (the Republic of China) and operates both domestic and international services.

Low-cost Lucky Air was founded in 2004 and based at Kunming, Yunnan province. It is now part of the Hainan Airlines group of companies. Seen on approach to Phuket International Airport, Thailand, in February 2017, is Boeing 737-808 B-5449 c/n 34971.

The holiday island of Hainan is the headquarters of Hainan Airlines, one of the largest privately owned carriers in China. It has an extensive route network, both domestic and international, and owns a number of other airlines that operate under their own names. Seen arriving at its gate at Bangkok Suvarnabhumi Airport, in November 2018, is Boeing 737-84P B-1495 c/n 63614.

Based at Osaka, JAL Express was a subsidiary of Japan Airlines. Pictured at a wet Naha Airport, Okinawa, in October 2004, is Boeing 737-446 JA8994 c/n 28097. Ten years later, in 2014, the carrier was merged into the parent company.

Japan TransOcean Air (JTA) is a member of the Japan Airlines group and is based on the southern island of Okinawa. Seen on pushback from its gate at its Naha Airport base, in October 2004, is Boeing 737-4K5 JA8934 c/n 27830.

Miyazaki-based Skynet Asia Airways (SNA) first operated services in 2002. Pictured at Tokyo Haneda Airport, in October 2004, is Boeing 737-4Y0 JA737E c/n 26069. In July 2011, the airline was rebranded as Solaseed Air.

Operating leased Kyrgyzstan-registered Boeing 737-2Q8 EX-006 c/n 21960 is Aero Asia International. The carrier was based in Karachi, Pakistan. The aircraft is pictured at Sharjah International Airport, UAE, in January 2006. In May of the following year, the company suspended operations.

Named after the city of its base, Zhongyuan Airlines was founded in 1986. Pictured at Shanghai Hongqiao International Airport, in October 1999, is Boeing 737-37K B-2574 c/n 29407. The following year, the company was taken over and absorbed into China Southern Airlines.

Landing at the old Guangzhou Baiyun International Airport, in October 1999, is Boeing 737-3W0 B-2983 c/n 28973 of Kunming-based China Yunnan Airlines. It was taken over and merged into China Eastern Airlines in 2002. In 2004, this airport closed and a new, much larger one opened using the same name.

Air Great Wall Boeing 737-2T4 B-2507 c/n 23273 is pictured at Beijing Capital International Airport in October 1999. The carrier flew domestic passenger services from its base at Ningbo, but it was taken over and merged into China Eastern Airlines in 2002.

Like many Chinese airlines, Wuhan Airlines was founded and based in the city of its name. Pictured on the move at Shanghai Hongqiao International Airport, in October 1999, is Boeing 737-3Q8 B-2919 c/n 24987. In August 2003, the carrier was taken over and merged into China Eastern Airlines.

Wearing special dolphin markings at Tokyo Haneda Airport, in October 2004, is Boeing 737-4Y0 JA319K c/n 24545 of Air Nippon (ANK). The company was a wholly owned subsidiary of All Nippon Airways. In April 2012, the carrier was merged into ANA Wings.

Boeing 737-54K JA8595 c/n 28461 has the standard Air Nippon livery. It is pictured, in October 2004, at a wet Naha Airport, Okinawa, so wet that it is fully reflected on the ground.

Approaching to land on Runway 19R at Bangkok Suvarnabhumi Airport, in March 2019, is Boeing 737-8LW B-1129 c/n 42971 of Hebei Airlines. Founded in 2010, the carrier is named after the regional province it is based in. Bangkok was the carrier's first international service.

T'way Air is a Seoul-based low-cost operator founded in 2010. Pictured at Da Nang International Airport, Vietnam, in March 2018, is Boeing 737-8Q8 HL8220 c/n 37162. It is of note that the company name on the cabin roof is in lower case lettering as 't'way'.

Few airliners have had as much influence on both airlines and passengers as the Boeing 747, forever known as the 'jumbo jet'. It was the first wide-body aircraft to see passenger service starting in 1970. Seen arriving at its gate at Bangkok Suvarnabhumi Airport, in November 2013, is Boeing 747-409 B-18211 of Taipei-based China Airlines.

As well as passengers, the 747 was also built as a dedicated cargo aircraft. Pictured landing at Frankfurt Airport, in July 2017, is Boeing 747-4FT(F) B-2475 c/n 34239 of Air China Cargo. This is the dedicated freight division of the Chinese flag carrier. The 747-400 series cargo version does not have the stretched upper deck of the passenger variant and, of course, any windows on the lower deck.

Seconds from touchdown at Tianjin Binhai International Airport, in November 2012, is Boeing 747-4B5(F) HL7467 c/n 27073 of Korean Air Cargo. This location is a major port city and the principal port for northern China and the capital Beijing.

Climbing out of Runway 01R at Bangkok Suvarnabhumi Airport, in November 2010, is Boeing 747-45E B-16405 c/n 27142 of Eva Air. This company is a major Taiwanese carrier, operating to worldwide locations as well as services to the Chinese mainland.

The final version of the 747 is the -8 variant. The fuselage was stretched, and it first flew in 2010. The freighter version has outsold the passenger configured aircraft by two to one. Pictured at Bangkok Suvarnabhumi Airport, in January 2020, is Boeing 747-8KZ(F) JA18KZ c/n 3614 of Nippon Cargo Airlines, a Tokyo-based all-cargo airline with worldwide services.

On approach to land at Tokyo Narita International Airport, in October 2004, is Boeing 747-246B JA8150 c/n 22479. It is operated by JALways, the charter division of Japan Airlines. It wears the special Reso'cha livery. The carrier was merged into the parent company in December 2010.

Japanese airlines often paint the whole aircraft in special colour schemes. This Boeing 747-481(D) JA8964 c/n 27163 of All Nippon Airways is pictured at Tokyo Haneda Airport, in October 2004, and is designed to advertise 'Pocket Monsters', also known as Pokémon. This 747 is one of the Japanese-only 'domestic jumbos'. In Japan, some 747s are used for internal flights of short distances but with high capacity, over 500 seats. Since most 747s operate long-hauls, the 'domestic' had a strengthened undercarriage, as it makes a lot more landings. The -400 'domestic' variant does not have the winglets, as they are of use mainly in long high-altitude cruising. These conditions do not apply to short internal services.

The Boeing 757 was the manufacturer's design to replace the 727. It first flew in February 1982 and was the first Boeing airliner launched with a foreign engine, this being the Rolls-Royce RB211. Sunday Airlines is a Kazakhstani charter carrier operating holiday flights. It is a subsidiary of Service Cargo Air Transport. Seen on approach to Astana International Airport, in June 2016, is Boeing 757-21B UP-B5703 c/n 25259.

As with the USSR (Union of Soviet Socialist Republics) and Aeroflot, all Chinese civil airliners were once operated by Civil Aviation Administration of China (CAAC). Today, there is a positive plethora of different carriers in that country. Boeing 757-21B B-2804 c/n 24330 of CAAC is at Bangkok Don Muang International Airport, in November 1989. At that time, it was the only airport in the city.

Pictured on the ramp at its base at Ürümqi Diwopu International Airport, in the far west of China, in October 1999, is Boeing 757-28C B-2859 c/n 29217 operated by China Xinjiang Airlines. The carrier was taken over by China Southern Airlines in 2003 and absorbed into its fleet.

Eva Air Boeing 757-27A B-27021 c/n 29611 is seen arriving at Macau International Airport in February 2003. Macau is an ex-Portuguese colony and, from 1999, a Special Administrative Region of the People's Republic of China. It is renowned for its casinos and is often called the 'Las Vegas of Asia'.

Shanghai Airlines Boeing 757-2D6 B-2843 c/n 27681 is about to line up to take-off at the new Guangzhou Baiyun International Airport in November 2012.

Air Astana Boeing 757-2G5 P4-FAS c/n 29489 taxies out to depart Astana International Airport in June 2016. The flag carrier of Kazakhstan, all the carrier's aircraft are registered in the Caribbean nation of Aruba, hence the 'P4' not 'UP' number.

The Boeing 767 first took to the air in September 1981 and was one of the first twin-engine, wide-body jets. MIAT-Mongolian Airlines Boeing 767-3WO(ER) JU-1012 c/n 28264 is on the runway at Berlin's Tegel Airport in September 2012. This location closed in November 2020.

Landing at Tianjin Binhai International Airport, in November 2012, is Asiana Cargo Boeing 767-38EF(ER) HL7507 c/n 25761. The Seoul-based carrier has a number of dedicated freight-only aircraft in their fleet.

Pictured on approach to Runway 19R at Bangkok Suvarnabhumi Airport, in March 2019, is Boeing 767-381F(ER) JA604F c/n 35709 operated by ANA Cargo, which is part of All Nippon Airways. As can be seen, the dedicated cargo variant of the 767 does not have cabin windows.

This November 1989 picture of China Airways Boeing 767-209 B-1836 c/n 23913 at Bangkok Don Muang International Airport shows the old-style livery of the Taipei-based carrier.

Air Do (Hokkaido International Airlines) Boeing 767-33A(ER) JA98AD c/n 27476 is on the move at Tokyo Haneda Airport in October 2004. The carrier is based in the north of Japan at Sapporo and offers a low-cost, high-density service to the capital.

To fill the gap in the market between the 747 and the 767, Boeing produced the 777. It was also mindful of the new technology being offered by Airbus with the A330 and A340 models. It first flew in June 1994. Pictured on approach, in November 2012, at Beijing Capital International Airport is Boeing 777-39L(ER) B-2035 c/n 38674 of Air China. It has the special livery of 'Smiling China', with portraits of smiling people on the rear fuselage.

Flying the dedicated freight version of the 777 is China Southern Cargo with Boeing 777-F1B B-2081 c/n 37313 at Frankfurt Airport in July 2017.

On the move at Tokyo Haneda Airport, in November 2014, is Boeing 777-381(ER) JA787A c/n 37949 of All Nippon Airways.

On approach to Hong Kong Chek Lap Kok Airport, in January 2013, is Boeing 777-267 B-HNA c/n 27265 of Cathay Pacific Airways. Based at this location, it is the largest carrier in the Special Administrative Region of Hong Kong and has scheduled passenger and cargo operations to worldwide locations.

Airliners of East and Central Asia

Pictured pushing back at Bangkok Suvarnabhumi Airport, in February 2013, is Boeing 777-35E (ER) B-16703 c/n 32643 of Taiwan-based Eva Air. As do many aircraft in Asia, it features a special livery, this one being the Sanrio family of characters. Sanrio is the largest manufacturer of greetings cards in Japan, and amongst the cartoon lines is the Hello Kitty one.

Lined up to land on Runway 09L at London Heathrow Airport, in July 2018, is Boeing 777-22K (LR) EZ-A779 c/n 42297 of Turkmenistan Airlines. Based in the capital city of Ashkhabad, it is the national flag carrier for the nation, which was once part of the USSR before its breakup in the 1990s.

The largest aircraft in the fleet of Seoul-based Jin Air is the 777, with 48 premium seats and 345 economy. The premium seats are the same size as the economy ones, but with 5in extra leg room. Pictured at Da Nang International Airport, Vietnam, in March 2018, is Boeing 777-2B5(ER) HL7743 c/n 34208.

Japan Airlines Boeing 777-246(ER) JA707J c/n 32894 is being pushed back at Tokyo Haneda Airport in November 2014.

The latest all-new design from Boeing is the 787, known as the Dreamliner. It first flew December 2009. It was late into service and was actually grounded by the FAA (Federal Aviation Authority) because of a number of fires due to the batteries used. The first carrier to put the type into service was All Nippon Airways. Pictured arriving at Düsseldorf International Airport, in August 2015, is Boeing 787-8 JA806A c/n 34515.

Seen arriving at Frankfurt Airport, in July 2017, is Boeing 787-9 JA864J c/n 34858 of Japan Airlines.

A subsidiary of Japan Airlines, Zip Air is a low-cost carrier based at Tokyo's Narita International Airport. Boeing 787-8 JA825J c/n 34835 is pictured on the move, in January 2020, at Bangkok Suvarnabhumi Airport. The official start-up of the company was planned for later in 2020 but was delayed by the COVID-19 pandemic. Another issue that has come into play is the Russian invasion of Ukraine. The airline has the single letter 'Z' on the fin, and this letter has also been used by the Russian military vehicles and tanks to mark who they are. To distance themselves from this, the Japanese carrier has removed the 'Z' and replaced it with a logo.

Turning into its gate at Bangkok Suvarnabhumi Airport, in January 2020, is Boeing 787-9 B-17881 c/n 39295 of Eva Air.

Wearing a special livery, Boeing 787-8 B-2727 c/n 34925 of China Southern Airlines approaches to land on Runway 09L at London Heathrow Airport in July 2018.

The Brazilian Embraer Regional Jet (ERJ)-145 first flew in August 1995 and has capacity for 50 passengers. In 2003, Embraer entered a partnership with the Harbin Aircraft Industry Group to assemble the ERJ-145. All the parts were sent in a 'knocked down' set of kits, and over 40 airframes were assembled in the northern Chinese city of Harbin. Pictured awaiting its next load of passengers at Xi'an Xianyang International Airport, in November 2012, is Embraer ERJ-145-LI B-3051 c/n 14500898 of China Eastern Airlines; this is a Harbin-assembled aircraft.

On approach to land at Tianjin Binhai International Airport, in November 2012, is Chinese-assembled Embraer ERJ-145-LI B-3085 c/n 14501047 of locally based Tianjin Airlines. The carrier operates to over 100 locations around China. It is part of the Hainan group of airlines.

Harbin-assembled Grand China Express Airlines Embraer ERJ-145-LI B-3082 c/n 14501030 is about to touch down at Tianjin Binhai International Airport in November 2012. The airline had been rebranded as Tianjin Airlines in June 2009, but this airframe had not yet been repainted.

Embraer expanded its range of airliners starting with the 70-seat E170, calling them the E-Jet family. From this came the E175, E190 and, the largest, the E195. The newest version can seat over 100 passengers depending upon the airlines' own layout. Seen pushing back, in November 2012, at Xi'an Xianyang International Airport, is Embraer 190LR B-3136 c/n 19000513 of China Southern Airlines.

On the move to the active runway at Astana International Airport, in June 2016, is Embraer 190-100LR P4-KCH c/n 19000547 of locally based Air Astana. Like all its fleet, the Kazakhstan flag carrier has its aircraft registered in Aruba.

Embraer 190AR B-16822 c/n 19000091 of Mandarin Airlines is on final approach to Hong Kong Chek Lap Kok Airport in January 2013. The carrier is from the Republic of China and based in Taipei, Taiwan. It operates scheduled passenger services around its island home, as well as regional international operations.

Developed from the Challenger business jet, the Canadair CRJ (Regional Jet) first flew in May 1991. China Eastern Airlines Canadair CRJ-200ER B-3013 c/n 7571 is pictured wearing a special livery as it lines up to land at Hong Kong Chek Lap Kok Airport in January 2013.

Landing at Astana International Airport, in June 2016, is Canadair CRJ-200LR UP-CJ005 c/n 7902 of Service Cargo Air Transport.

J Air operates feeder flights for Japan Airlines. Seen at Osaka Itami International Airport, in October 2004, is Canadair CRJ-200ER JA201J c/n 7452.

IBEX Airlines provides feeder connections for All Nippon Airways and carries ANA Connection titles, as well as its own. Pictured at Miyazaki Airport, in October 2014, is Canadair CRJ-702ER JA06RJ c/n 10303. The -700 series was first flown in May 1999 and was a stretched development from the -200.

The CRJ was further stretched to produce the -900, which first flew in February 2001 and could seat up to 90 passengers. Pictured, in February 2018, at Bangkok Don Muang International Airport is Canadair CRJ-900LR B-3379 c/n 15368 of China Express Airlines. The carrier is the nation's first privately owned regional airline and operates to over 70 destinations from its base in the city of Chongqing.

One of the best-selling and widely used aircraft is the de Havilland Canada-built Dash-8. First flown in June 1983, the twin turboprop has excellent short field performance. Under tow at Okinawa's Naha Airport, in October 2004, is de Havilland Canada DHC-8-103 Dash-8 JA8974 c/n 540 operated by Ryukyu Air Commuter (RAC). The carrier, which is based at this location, is owned by Japan TransOcean Air and operates domestic services to the local islands.

Oriental Air Bridge is based in the city of Nagasaki and operates charter flights, as well as limited domestic services. On the move at Nagasaki Airport, in October 2004, is de Havilland Canada DHC-8-201 Dash-8 JA801B c/n 566.

The ultimate development of the Dash 8 is the -400 series. It is 34ft (10.36m) longer, has much more powerful engines and can seat 74 passengers. It first flew in January 1998. Climbing out of Miyazaki Airport, in October 2014, is de Havilland Canada DHC-8 Dash 8-Q400 JA845C c/n 4101 of Japan Air Commuter. The carrier's role is to provide feeder services for its parent company, Japan Airlines.

One of the best-selling British-designed post-war aircraft is the Britten-Norman Islander. First flown in June 1965, it was able to operate almost anywhere in the world. It has a fixed undercarriage and simple features to aid maintenance. Seen at Okinawa's Naha Airport, in October 2004, is Britten-Norman BN-2B Islander JA5324 c/n 2297 of locally based Ryukyu Air Commuter.

After a gap of some 30 years, Swedish manufacturer Saab returned to the production of civil aircraft. First flown in January 1983, the model 340 could seat up to 35 passengers. Pictured at Xi'an Xianyang International Airport, in October 1999, is Saab 340B B-3657 c/n 340B-357 operated by Shandong Airlines. Based in the city of Jinan and named after the province of Shandong, the carrier has an extensive network of domestic services, as well as limited regional international ones.

On the taxiway about to depart its Ürümqi Diwopu International Airport base is ATR 72-500 B-3022 c/n 521 of China Xinjiang Airlines. The aircraft's manufacturer, ATR (Avions de Transport Régional), is a joint venture between France's Aérospatiale and Italy's Aeritalia to build twin-engine turboprops for regional services. The airline was taken over by China Southern Airlines in 2004.

The MD-90 was one of the final developments from the original Douglas DC-9. Seen landing on a grey day, in November 2012, at Guangzhou Baiyun International Airport is McDonnell Douglas MD-90-30 B-17919 c/n 53569 of Uni Air. The carrier is Taiwanese and operates both domestic and regional international passenger services.

Pictured on the move at Osaki Itami International Airport, in October 2004, is McDonnell Douglas MD-90-30 JA001D c/n 53555 of Japan Air Systems (JAS). Two years later, the carrier was taken over and merged into Japan Airlines.

Landing at the old, now closed, Guangzhou Baiyun International Airport, in October 1999, is McDonnell Douglas MD-90-30 B-2256 c/n 53582 of China Eastern Airlines. The Shanghai-based carrier is one of the largest in the country.

First flown in August 1970, the Douglas DC-10 is a three-engine, wide-body, twin-aisle airliner. On the move at Nagoya Airport, in October 2004, is McDonnell Douglas DC-10-40 JA8534 c/n 46913 of national flag carrier Japan Airlines.

As a follow on from the DC-10, the manufacturer produced the MD-11. It was the first time that the new owners of the Douglas Aircraft Company used its own prefix, dropping the 'DC' (Douglas Commercial) that dated back to 1933. The new airliner first flew in January 1990. Seen climbing out from Runway 01R at Bangkok Suvarnabhumi Airport, in November 2010, is McDonnell Douglas MD-11(F) B-16109 c/n 48779 operated in a cargo role by Eva Air.

The MD-11 did not prove all that popular with a number of airlines, as it failed to live up to the range promised by the manufacturer. However, it has proved to be one of the most used cargo aircraft. Climbing out of Bangkok Suvarnabhumi Airport, in November 2010, is McDonnell Douglas MD-11(F) B-2179 c/n 45845 operated by Shanghai Airlines Cargo. Operations from China covered Europe and the US, as well as other Asian nations.

China Eastern Airlines operated its MD-11s either for passenger or cargo operations. On the move at the carrier's base of Shanghai Hongqiao International Airport, in October 1999, is McDonnell Douglas MD-11 B-2174 c/n 48498. This airframe is passenger configured.

First flying in November 1970, the Lockheed TriStar was the second three-engine, wide-body, twin-aisle airliner looking for customers around the world. Seen in the carrier's previous livery at Bangkok Don Muang International Airport, in November 1989, is Lockheed L-1011-385 TriStar 1 VR-HOC c/n 193A-1042 of Hong Kong-based Cathay Pacific Airways. At this time, Hong Kong was still a British colony, and the aircraft has the local 'VR-H..' registration. It was not until 1997 that it reverted to Chinese control.

The first airliner launched by British Aerospace was the BAe 146, and it first flew in September 1981. Despite having four engines, it was one of the quietest airliners flying. On the move at Lanzhou Zhongchuan International Airport, in October 1999, is BAe 146-100 B-2703 c/n E1032 of Xian-based China Northwest Airlines. In 2002, the carrier was merged into China Eastern Airlines.

Awaiting its next load of passengers at the old Guangzhou Baiyun International Airport, in October 1999, is BAe 146-100 B-2710 c/n E1085 in the livery of Air China.

To bring the old F.27 Friendship turboprop design up to date, the Dutch manufacturer Fokker produced the F50. It first flew in December 1985. On the move at Nagoya Airport, in October 2004, is Fokker 50 JA8200 c/n 20307 of locally based Naka Nihon Air Line (NAL). In February the following year, the carrier was rebranded as Air Central.

Fokker also updated its F.28 Fellowship jet by producing the F70 and the larger F100. Pictured arriving at Astana International Airport, in June 2016, is Fokker 100 UP-F1005 c/n 11500 operated by Bek Air. The company was founded as Berkut Air to operate business jets and later moved to passenger operations with a new name. The Kazakhstan government closed the carrier down in 2020 due to many safety violations.

The Tupolev Tu-134 was designed in the USSR as a short-haul jet airliner and first took to the air in July 1963. On the ramp at Kalma International Airport, Wonsan, Democratic People's Republic of Korea (better known as North Korea), in September 2016, is Tupolev Tu-134B P-813 c/n 66215 in the smart livery of Air Koryo, the only airline in the country.

Soviet-designed for the medium-range market, the Tu-154 first flew in October 1968. Pictured on the ramp at Sharjah International Airport, UAE, in March 1997, is Tupolev Tu-154B-2 EY-85475 c/n 475 of Tajik Air, based in Dushanbe, Tajikistan. This nation was one of several that broke away from the USSR when it collapsed to become an independent country.

Another former Soviet republic and now independent nation is Kazakhstan. Tupolev Tu-154B-2 UN-85396 c/n 396 of Kazakstan Airlines (note the spelling of the name on the cabin roof) is pictured at Sharjah International Airport in March 1997. The country's registration letter was originally 'UN' but since this caused confusion with the United Nations, it was changed to 'UP'. The carrier was renamed Air Kazakstan in 1997 but suspended operations in 2004, following mounting debts.

On approach to Frankfurt Airport, in June 2001, is Tupolev Tu-154 UN-85781 c/n 965 of Air Kazakstan (again, note the spelling of the name).

By the late 1990s, few airlines in China still operated the Soviet-era equipment. Pictured at the old Guangzhou Baiyun International Airport, in October 1999, is Tupolev Tu-154M B-2629 c/n 919 in service with Sichuan Airlines. The Chengdu-based company now has an all-Airbus fleet.

On the ramp at Kalma International Airport, Wonsan, North Korea, in September 2016, is Tupolev Tu-154B P-552 c/n 76A143 of Pyongyang-based Air Koryo. The carrier is one of the very few to have old Soviet-era aircraft still in passenger service.

Tupolev Tu-154B P-561 c/n 83A573 of Air Koryo has its engines covered at the carrier's Pyongyang International Airport base in September 2016. This example still has the old-style livery. Much of the fleet will sit idle for long periods, as the airline has so few flights either domestic or international.

On the move to the active runway is Tupolev Tu-154B-2 EX-85497 c/n 497 of Kyrghyzstan Airlines at Sharjah International Airport in March 2000. Based in the capital Bishkek, the carrier was declared bankrupt in 2005 and ceased operations. Kyrghyzstan was once part of the USSR and is now officially known as the Kyrgyz Republic.

China Xinjiang Airlines was one of the last operators of Soviet-built airliners in China. On the ramp at the carrier's base at Ürümqi Diwopu International Airport in the far west of that vast nation is Tupolev Tu-154M B-2611 c/n 726. It is pictured in October 1999.

Retired out of service and in store awaiting sale, in October 1999, is Tupolev Tu-154M B-2623 c/n 855 of China Northwest Airlines at the carrier's Xi'an Xianyang International Airport base. In 2002, the company was merged into China Eastern Airlines.

First flown in January 1989, the Tu-204 was designed to replace the many Tu-154s in service. By the time all the test flying had been completed, the political map had changed, and the USSR no longer existed. In the 'new' Russia and the republics that had split away, the newly formed airlines could, and did, buy and lease Western-built airliners, so the Tu-204 has had only limited success. Seen on pushback at its Pyongyang International Airport base, in September 2016, is Tupolev Tu-204-300 P-632 c/n 1450742364012 of Air Koryo.

Air Koryo is one of the last, if not the last, passenger operator of the Ilyushin IL-18. A four-engine turboprop that first flew in 1957, a few still fly cargo in underdeveloped parts of the world. Ilyushin IL-18D P-835 c/n 188011205 is at Kalma International Airport, Wonsan, in September 2016.

The IL-62 is a Soviet long-range airliner with four rear-mounted engines, very few of which still fly today. On the ramp at Moscow Zhukovsky International Airport, in August 1995, is Ilyushin IL-62M UN-86130 c/n 3255333 of Aral Air from Kazakhstan. The carrier only operated from 1991 to 2002, when services were suspended.

Still in a full two-class passenger configuration is Ilyushin IL-62M P-885 c/n 3933913 of Air Koryo at Kalma International Airport, Wonsan, in September 2016.

The IL-76 is one of the most widely used and versatile cargo aircraft operating today. It first took to the air in March 1971. On the ramp at Sharjah International Airport, UAE, in March 1997, is Ilyushin IL-76TD UK 76793 c/n 0093498951 operated by Tashkent-based Uzbekistan Airways. The airline is the ex-Soviet republic's flag carrier.

A sight unlikely to be seen often outside its North Korean border is Ilyushin IL-76TD P-913 c/n 1003404126 of Air Koryo. It is pictured on the ramp at Kalma International Airport, Wonsan, in September 2016.

The first Soviet wide-body was the IL-86, and it was quite underpowered. Operating a passenger service at Sharjah International Airport, in March 2000, is Ilyushin IL-86 UK 86056 c/n 51483203023 operated by Uzbekistan Airways. It is configured with a 350-all economy seating layout.

Only one Chinese carrier operated the IL-86 Soviet wide-body. On the move at Shanghai Hongqiao International Airport, in October 1999, is Ilyushin IL-86 B-2016 c/n 51483210097 of China Xinjiang Airlines.

The Yakovlev Yak-40 is a regional airliner with three rear-mounted engines. It first flew in October 1966 and had a seating capacity of up to 32 passengers. Seen on the ramp at Astana International Airport, in June 2016, is Yakovlev Yak-40K UP-Y4028 c/n 9710453 of East Wing, based at this location. The company is a cargo charter carrier.

Climbing out of Astana International Airport, in June 2016, is Yakovlev Yak-40K UP-Y4019 c/n 9741855 of Zhetysu Aviakompania. The carrier provides passenger charter services from its base in the Kazakhstan city of Taldykorgan.

The first prototype of the Yak-42 flew in March 1975. With three rear-mounted engines, it was a medium-range airliner. Pictured arriving at the old Guangzhou Baiyun International Airport, in October 1999, is Yakovlev Yak-42D B-2754 c/n 4520423116579 of China General Aviation. Based in Shanxi province, the carrier operated a variety of types in such roles as utility and photo survey, as well as passenger services. The previous year, it was taken over by China Eastern Airlines, but this aircraft had not yet been repainted in the new owner's livery.

With both turboprops running, Antonov An-24B UP-AN404 c/n 17307303 operated by Service Cargo Air Transport, is pictured on arrival at Astana International Airport, in June 2016. The An-24 first flew in December 1962 and was the USSR's replacement for the older piston types still in service.

On the ramp at Samjiyon Airport, in September 2016, is Antonov An-24B P-537 c/n 67302408 of Air Koryo. The aircraft was on a domestic service from Wonsan, later flying on to the capital, Pyongyang.

China licence-built the An-24 as the Xian Y-7 and later updated the design. On the move at Xi'an Xianyang International Airport, in October 1999, is Xian Y-7-200A B-3720 c/n 0001 of locally based carrier Changan Air, now rebranded as Chang'An Airlines. This variant has been equipped with Western-built engines for better performance.

On approach to land at Xi'an Xianyang International Airport, in November 2012, is Aviation Industry Corporation of China (AVIC) MA-60 B-3455 c/n 0803 of locally based Joy Air. The carrier operates scheduled passenger services around northwest China. The MA-60 is a development of the Y-7 by Aviation Industry Corporation of China. The 'MA' stands for 'Modern Ark', and the '60' is for the maximum seating capacity.

The latest development of the MA-60 is an all-freight version. Pictured at Zhuhai Jinwan Airport, in November 2012, is Aviation Industry Corporation of China MA-600F B-200L c/n RK-109 in the manufacturer's livery. The large cargo door can be seen clearly.

Another Soviet design built under licence in China is the Antonov An-2, known as the Y-5. Pictured on take-off from Lanzhou Zhongchuan International Airport, in October 1999, is Yunshuji Y-5 B-8238 c/n 316409 operated by locally based China Northwest Airlines. One of its roles was that of crop spraying, and its wing tips have been modified. These are known as 'tipsails' and change the aircraft's wake when spraying.

First flown in December 1974, the Y-8 is a Chinese-built version of the Antonov An-12. The main visual difference is the longer nose on the Chinese aircraft. Landing at the old Guangzhou Baiyun International Airport, in October 1999, is Yunshuji Y-8F-100 B-3102 c/n 50805 of Tianjin-based China Postal Airlines. As the name suggests, the airline operates for the Ministry of Posts.

China has, of course, produced some aircraft that have been designed and built in the country. One of the first to go into production was the Y-11. It is an eight-seat utility aircraft powered by a pair of radial piston engines. Pictured in October 1999, at Shihezi Airfield, and operated by the Xinjiang General Aviation Company is Harbin Yunshuji Y-11 B-3894 c/n 0310.

Developed from the Y-11, the Y-12 had a longer fuselage that could seat 17 passengers and was now powered by a pair of turboprop engines. Harbin Yunshuji Y-12 B-3817 c/n 0029 is operated by Xinjiang General Aviation Company and is pictured at Shihezi Airfield in October 1999.

The latest version of the Y-12 is a new-generation multi-role turboprop designed and built by Aviation Industry Corporation of China. It can seat up to 19 passengers and has a new 'glass' cockpit instrumentation display. Aviation Industry Corporation of China Harbin Y-12F B-1233L is in the manufacturer's livery at Zhuhai Jinwan Airport in November 2012.

The ARJ21 (Advanced Regional Jet) is the latest airliner to be designed and built in China. It can seat up to 90 passengers and is now in service. Comac ARJ21-700 B-992L c/n 103 is in the manufacturer's colours at Zhuhai Jinwan Airport in November 2012.

Pictured on the ramp at Sharjah International Airport, in March 2000, is Antonov An-12B UK 11369 c/n 6343810 of Tashkent-based Uzbekistan Airways. The An-12 is the Soviet equivalent of the Lockheed Hercules and can be found in both civil and military markings, hauling cargo in many parts of the world.

With its aircraft registered in the former Soviet republic of Kyrgyzstan, Reem Air's main operating base was in the United Arab Emirates. Seen at Sharjah International Airport, in January 2006, is Antonov An-12 EX-098 c/n 401912 with Reem Air titles and the Kyrgyz Republic flag on the nose. The all-cargo carrier suspended operations the following year.

When the USSR split into the different republics, one of the major aircraft manufactures of the Soviet era was Antonov, which is based in the now independent Ukraine. It has continued to design and build airliners. The An-148 is a regional jet that first flew in December 2004. On the ramp at Pyongyang International Airport, with its engines and cockpit covered, in September 2016, is Antonov An-148B P-671 c/n 0308 of locally based carrier Air Koryo. The An-148 is the most modern design in Air Koryo's fleet.

Mongolian Airlines was formed in 2011, and, owing to confusion with the national flag carrier, MIAT-Mongolian Airlines, it changed its name to Hunnu Air in 2013. Pictured on approach to Hong Kong Chek Lap Kok Airport, in January 2013, is Airbus A319-112 JU-8888 c/n 1706 in the carrier's most attractive livery.

The single-aisle Airbus range of the A319/320/321 has become the most successful jet airliner of all time in terms of sales, and the manufacturer has a huge backlog of orders to fulfil. On the runway at Tianjin Binhai International Airport, in November 2012, is the smallest of the current range produced, Airbus A319-132 B-6421 c/n 4995 operated by West Air, a low-cost carrier based in Chongqing.

On approach to land at Xi'an Xianyang International Airport, in November 2012, is Airbus A319-112 B-6169 c/n 2985 of Capital Airlines. The company operates scheduled domestic services from its Beijing base.

The smallest aircraft in flag carrier Air China's fleet is the A319. They are configured with eight business class and 120 economy seats. Pictured about to land at Xi'an Xianyang International Airport, in November 2012, is Airbus A319-132 B-6024 c/n 2015.

The second in the single-aisle range is the A320. Tianjin Airlines Airbus A320-232 B-6837 c/n 4825 is pictured at Xi'an Xianyang International Airport, in November 2012. The airline operates scheduled passenger services from its base in the city of the same name.

Shanghai-based Juneyao Airlines (now Air) operates to over 70 cities around mainland China. Airbus A320-214 B-6602 c/n 3984 is seen at Xi'an Xianyang International Airport in November 2012.

All Nippon Airways Airbus A320-211 JA8392 c/n 328 is pictured at Miyazaki Airport, in October 2014, on a domestic service.

Airbus A320-271N B-LCN c/n 7512 of Hong Kong Express Airways is on approach to land at Phuket International Airport, Thailand, in February 2020. The carrier is a low-cost company owned by Cathay Pacific Airways.

Shanghai-based Spring Airlines is a low-cost carrier that operates both domestic and regional international passenger services and charters. On the runway, in October 2014, at Ibaraki Hyakuri Airport, Japan, a mixed civil and military airfield, is Airbus A320-214 B-6970 c/n 5403.

Shenzhen Airlines is based in the city of the same name. It operates both domestic and international services. Airbus A320-232 B-6720 c/n 4474 is on approach to land at Xi'an Xianyang International Airport in November 2012.

Sporting a special colour scheme to advertise a horticultural exposition, China Eastern Airlines Airbus A320-214 B-6028 c/n 2171 is landing at Hong Kong Chek Lap Kok Airport in January 2013.

Hong Kong Airlines is part of the Hainan Airlines group of companies. Seen in January 2013, Airbus A320-214 B-LPG c/n 5266 is arriving at the carrier's base at Chek Lap Kok Airport.

Based in the city of the same name, Chongqing Airlines is 60 per cent owned by China Southern Airlines. The carrier operates mainly domestic services, as well as a few regional international ones. Pictured at the new Guangzhou Baiyun International Airport, in November 2012, is Airbus A320-233 B-2343 c/n 696.

First flown in March 1993, the A321 is the longest of the single-aisle Airbus range. On its way to the active runway at Beijing Capital International Airport, in November 2012, is Airbus A321-231 B-6551 c/n 3730 of Chengdu-based Sichuan Airlines.

China Southern Airlines Airbus A321-231 B-6658 c/n 4271 is pictured on approach to Hong Kong Chek Lap Kok Airport in January 2013. The carrier operates the A321 in a three-class configuration, with 12 business, 24 premium economy and 143 economy seats.

Airbus A321-231 HL8257 c/n 5173 of Seoul-based Asiana Airlines is about to land at Hong Kong Chek Lap Kok Airport in January 2013. This company has a two-class layout, with 12 business and 165 economy seats.

Landing at Beijing Capital International Airport, in September 2016, is Airbus A321-231 B-MBB c/n 5523 of Air Macau. Macau was a Portuguese colony that reverted to Chinese control in December 1999.

On pushback at Bangkok Don Muang International Airport, in January 2015, is Airbus A321-231 B-22608 c/n 6009 of V-Air. The carrier was short lived; it commenced operations in December 2014 and ceased them in October 2016. Based in Taiwan, it was a low-cost franchise of TransAsia Airways.

About to land on Runway 09 at Phuket International Airport, Thailand, in January 2019, is Airbus A321-231 B-HTF c/n 633 of Hong Kong-based Cathay Dragon Airlines. The company was owned by Cathay Pacific Airways, and, owing to the outbreak of COVID-19, the carrier was closed down by its parent company and ceased all operations in October 2020.

On the ramp at Macau International Airport, in February 2003, is Airbus A321-131 B-22606 c/n 731 of Taiwanese-based TransAsia Airways. The carrier ceased operations in March 2016.

Hong Kong-based Dragon Air Airbus A321-231 B-HTK c/n 3669 is pictured on approach to Phuket International Airport, Thailand, in February 2017. In November of the previous year, the carrier had been rebranded as Cathay Dragon, but this airframe had not yet been repainted.

First flying in November 1992, the A330 is a very popular twin-engine, twin-aisle, wide-body for medium- to long-haul routes. Wearing a special livery at its Beijing Capital International Airport base, in November 2012, is Airbus A330-243 B-6075 c/n 785 of Air China.

Having been pushed back from its gate, China Southern Airlines Airbus A330-223 B-6522 c/n 1244 is ready to depart to the runway at Frankfurt Airport in July 2017.

On the runway at Tokyo Haneda Airport, in October 2014, is Airbus A330-343 JA330B c/n 1491 of locally based Skymark Airlines. The A330 was the largest aircraft in its fleet, but it has since sold them all.

Pictured climbing out of Manchester Airport, in May 2018, is Airbus A330-343 B-1021 c/n 1831 of Hainan Airlines. It is one of the longer routes the carrier operates.

Wearing a special livery to advertise an event in its home base city of Shanghai is Airbus A330-343 B-6100 c/n 928 of China Eastern Airlines. It is pictured on approach to Hong Kong Chek Lap Kok Airport in January 2013.

South Korea-based Asiana Airlines Airbus A330-323 HL7741 c/n 708 lines up to land at Hong Kong Chek Lap Kok Airport in January 2013.

China Airlines Airbus A330-302 B-18303 c/n 641 is on approach to Hong Kong Chek Lap Kok Airport, in January 2013. The Taiwan-based carrier has a very smart colour scheme.

To celebrate its 20th anniversary, Dragon Air painted Airbus A330-343 B-HWG c/n 662 in a wonderful livery showing the Chinese dragon. It is landing at Hong Kong Chek Lap Kok Airport in January 2013.

The flag carrier for Hong Kong is Cathay Pacific Airways, which operates both passenger and cargo services worldwide. Airbus A330-342 B-HLD c/n 102 heads back to its base at Chek Lap Kok Airport in January 2013.

In its distinctive blue colour scheme Korean Air Airbus A330-322 HL7524 c/n 206 is about to land at Hong Kong Chek Lap Kok Airport in January 2013.

From its base at Lhasa, Tibet Autonomous Region, Tibet Airlines operates domestic and limited international services. Pictured with the pushback tug attached as it gets ready to depart from Beijing Capital International Airport, in September 2016, is Airbus A330-243 B-8420 c/n 1730.

On approach to land on Runway 19R at Bangkok Suvarnabhumi Airport, in January 2013, is Airbus A330-203 B-16310 c/n 678 of Taipei-based Eva Air.

Heading for its gate upon arrival at Bangkok Suvarnabhumi Airport, in January 2019, is Airbus A330-343 B-LNU c/n 1124 of Hong Kong Airlines. The carrier is part of the Hainan Airlines group, and most of the companies have a common tail marking.

On finals to land at Phuket International Airport, Thailand, in January 2020, is Airbus A330-343 B-HYJ c/n 512 of Cathay Dragon Airlines. Owned by Cathay Pacific Airways, the airline closed down in October 2020.

First flown in October 1996, the A340 was the 'sister' aircraft to the A330 but with four engines for long-haul operations. On approach to Hong Kong Chek Lap Kok Airport, in January 2013, is Airbus A340-313 B-HXF c/n 160 of locally based Cathay Pacific Airways. This airframe is configured with 26 business class and 257 economy seats.

On pushback at Hong Kong Chek Lap Kok Airport, in March 2003, is Airbus A340-313 B-2383 c/n 161 of Shanghai-based China Eastern Airlines.

On the move at the old Guangzhou Baiyun International Airport, in October 1999, is Airbus A340-313 B-2388 c/n 242 of China Southwest Airlines. Chengdu-based, the carrier was taken over and merged into Air China in October 2002.

First flying in April 2001, the A340-600 series was much longer than the -300 model and had more powerful engines. Pictured on a dull day, in November 2012, at the new Guangzhou Baiyun International Airport is Airbus A340-642 B-6508 c/n 436 of Hainan Airlines.

With a full-length double-deck, the prototype A380 first flew in April 2005 and is the world's largest passenger airliner. Landing at Frankfurt Airport, in July 2017, is Airbus A380-841 HL7625 c/n 152 of Asiana Airlines.

Pictured having just landed on Runway 19R at Bangkok Suvarnabhumi Airport, in February 2017, is Airbus A380-861 HL7619 c/n 096 of Korean Air, the national flag carrier of South Korea.

About to land at Beijing Capital International Airport, in November 2012, is Airbus A380-841 B-6139 c/n 088 of China Southern Airlines. The carrier operates the aircraft in a three-class configuration, with eight first, 70 business and 428 economy seats.

The first Airbus design to enter production was the A300; the prototype first flew in October 1972. It was a twin-aisle, twin-engine, wide-body that could seat more than 300 passengers depending upon the airline. As development progressed, new improved variants were produced. Airbus A300B4-622R B-18571 c/n 529 of China Airlines is pictured arriving at its gate, in November 1999, at Bangkok Don Muang International Airport.

On pushback from its gate at Singapore Changi Airport, in February 2003, is Airbus A300-605R B-2307 c/n 525 of China Eastern Airlines. The carrier had configured this aircraft with 24 first class and 250 economy seats.

On the move at Tokyo Haneda Airport, in October 2004, is Airbus A300-622R JA8527 c/n 724 of Japan Air System. The carrier had been taken over in April of that year and rebranded as Japan Airlines Domestic. This airframe had not yet been repainted in the new livery.

Shorter than the A300 it was developed from, the A310 was the second design from Airbus, and it first flew in April 1982. Pictured on approach to Runway 27R at London Heathrow Airport, in June 1996, is Airbus A310-324 F-OGQZ c/n 576 of Tashkent-based Uzbekistan Airways. The aircraft was leased, hence the French registration.

Pictured at Shanghai Hongqiao International Airport, in October 1999, is Airbus A310-222 B-2301 c/n 311 of Xian-based China Northwest Airlines. In 2002, the carrier was taken over and merged into China Eastern Airlines.

The latest all-new design from Airbus is the A350. It first flew in June 2013 and entered service two years later. Pictured climbing out of Manchester Airport, in May 2018, is Airbus A350-941 B-LRK c/n 070 of Hong Kong-based Cathay Pacific Airways.

Heading for its gate at Bangkok Suvarnabhumi Airport, in January 2020, is Airbus A350-941 B-18917 c/n 208 of China Airlines. It has a sticker on the rear fuselage to celebrate 60 years of operation by the carrier, which was founded in 1959.

Airbus A350-941 B-18916 c/n 191 of China Airlines is at Bangkok Suvarnabhumi Airport in November 2018. This side view shows off the change in shape from the A330, especially around the nose and fin.

Other books you might like:

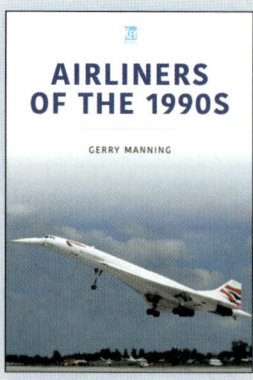

Historical Commercial Aircraft Series, Vol. 4

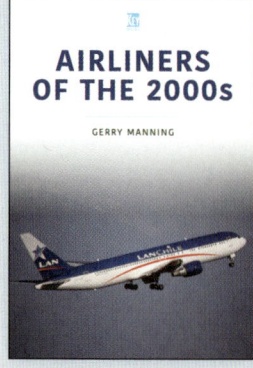

Historical Commercial Aircraft Series, Vol. 5

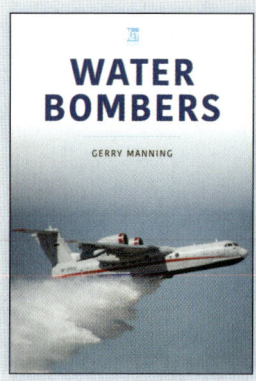

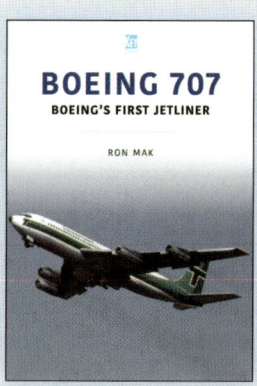

Historical Commercial Aircraft Series, Vol. 2

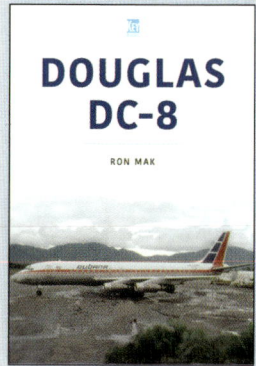

Historical Commercial Aircraft Series, Vol. 7

For our full range of titles please visit:
shop.keypublishing.com/books

VIP Book Club

Sign up today and receive TWO FREE E-BOOKS

Be the first to find out about our forthcoming book releases and receive exclusive offers.

Register now at **keypublishing.com/vip-book-club**

Our VIP Book Club is a 100% spam-free zone, and we will never share your email with anyone else. You can read our full privacy policy at: privacy.keypublishing.com